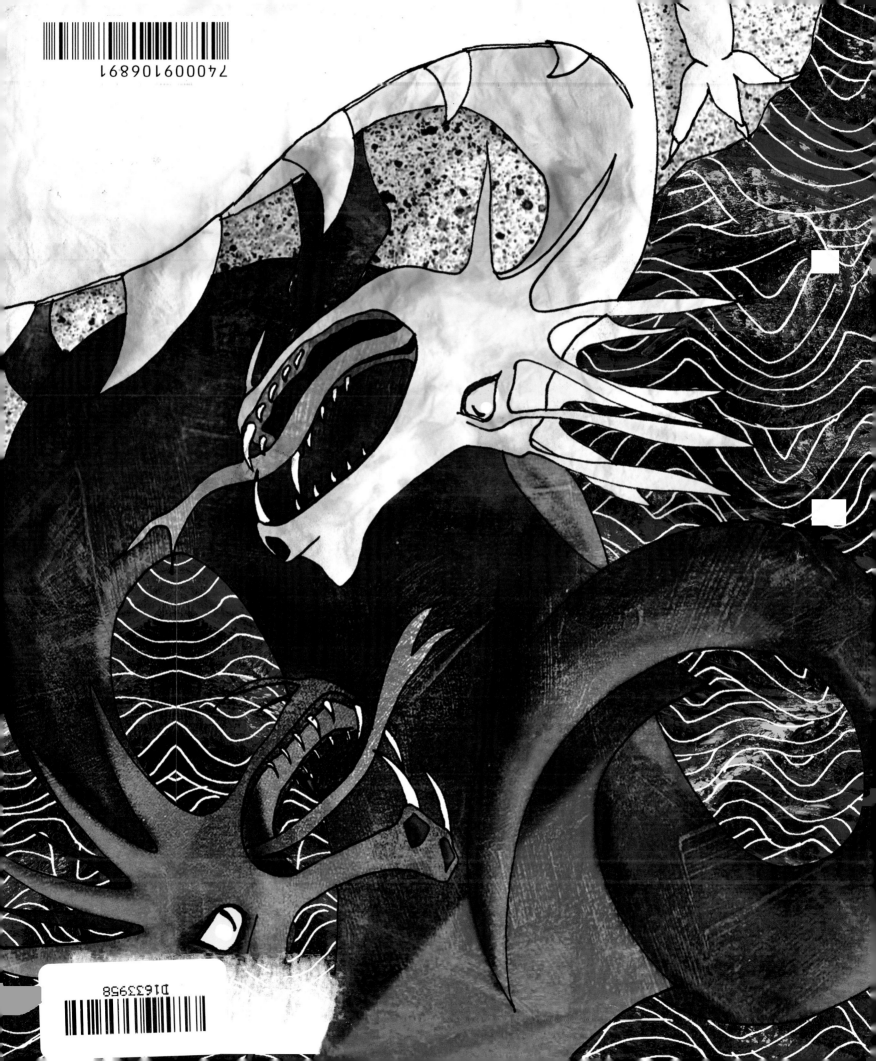

For Jeanne
Though we haven't travelled far,
we've usually travelled together.

**Pictures
to share**

First published in 2009 by
Pictures to Share Community Interest Company,
a UK based social enterprise that publishes
illustrated books for older people.

www.picturestoshare.co.uk

ISBN 978-0-9553940-7-2

Travelling
in pictures

Edited by Helen J Bate

A journey of a thousand miles begins with a single step

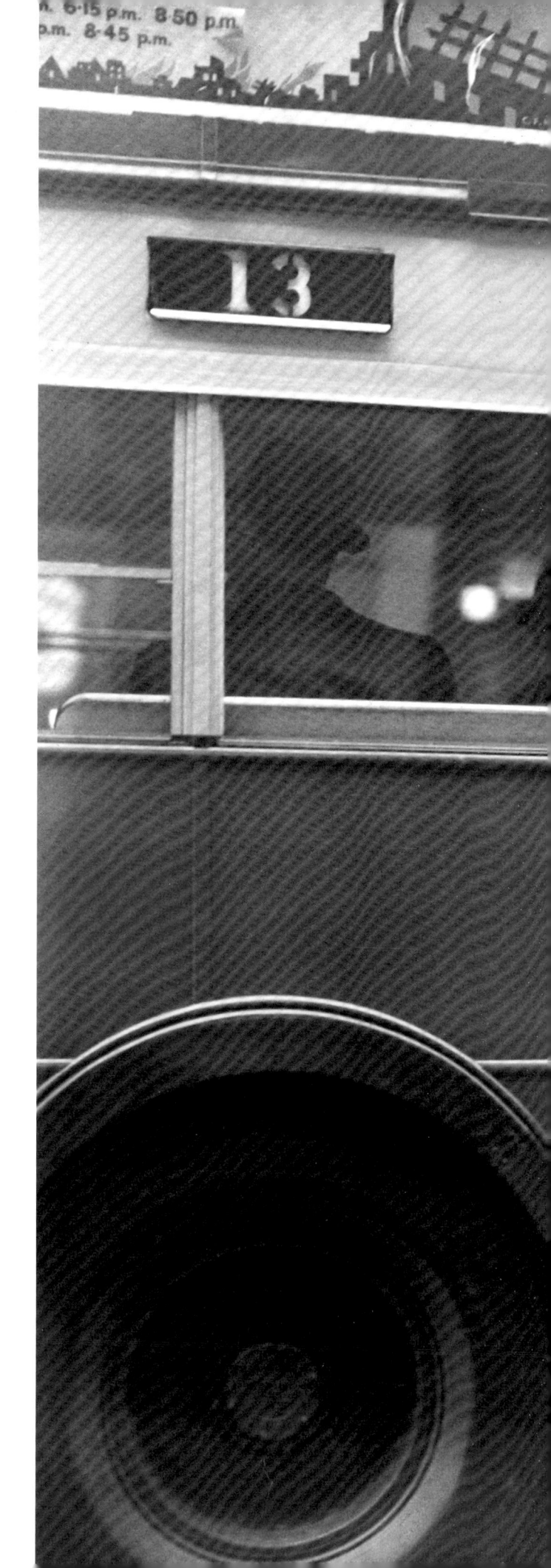

Photograph: A passenger jumps on board a moving London bus. © Hudson/Hulton Archive/Getty Images

Quotation: from 'The Way of Lao-tzu' by Lao-Tzu Chinese philosopher (604BC - 531BC)

One of the pleasantest
things in the world
is going on a journey;

but I like to go by myself

Painting: Going into the World (oil on canvas) by Evert Jan Boks,
Dutch Artist (1838-1914) Bridgeman Art Library/Getty Images

Quotation: from 'Going on a Journey' 1822 by William Hazlitt (1778-1830)

Since life is short, and the world is wide,

the sooner you start exploring it, the better.

We three kings of Orient are

Bearing gifts we travel afar
Field and fountain,
moor and mountain
Following yonder star

Just tea for two
And two for tea

I'm discontented with homes that I've rented
So I have invented my own.

Darling, this place is a lovely oasis
Where life's weary taste is unknown,

Far from the crowded city
Where flowers caress the stream

Cozy to hide in, to live side by side,
Don't let it abide in my dream.

Established in 1872,

Yellowstone National Park

was America's first national park.
Two species of bear live there;
the black bear and the grizzly bear.

Step with care and great tact
And remember that Life's

a Great Balancing Act

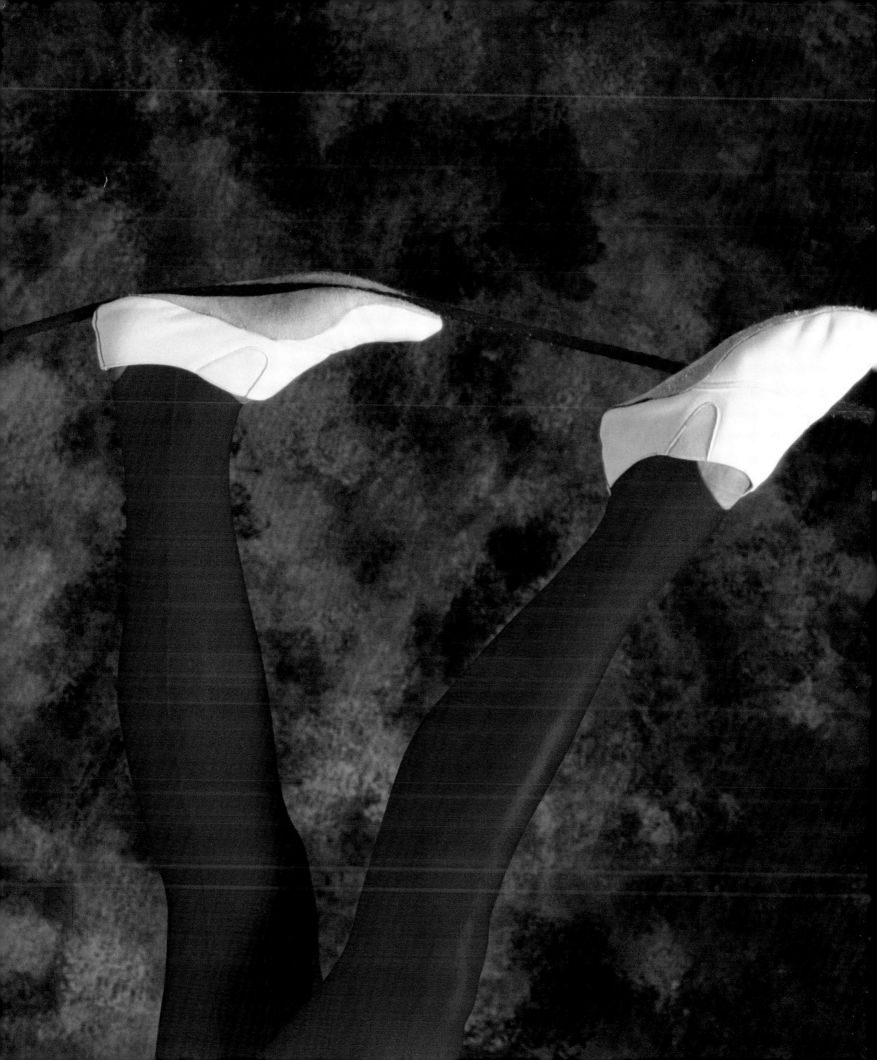

Sailing holidays

A family having tea
in the cabin of their boat
on the Norfolk Broads
in England.

A couple from the West Indies travel from

Southampton
to London Victoria

I'm driving home for

Christmas

In order for people
to be happy,

sometimes
they have to take risks.

Photograph: Climbers on the Eiger. © Louise Feinnes

Quotation: Meg Cabot, The Boy Next Door, 2002

Sittin' on the seat
of my stalled car,

Wondering what
my options are.

Think of
all the beauty
around you

and be happy.

Photograph: Dawn at the Taj Mahal, Uttar Pradesh, Agra, India
© Ed Freeman/Stone/Getty Images

Quotation: Anne Frank (1929 - 1945), Diary of a Young Girl, 1952
www.quotationspage.com

Photograph: Two policemen cycling down a flooded road in Berkshire.

© Topical Press Agency/Hulton Archive/Getty Images

No matter where you live,

brothers are brothers
and sisters are sisters.

The bonds that keep family close
are the same,
no matter where you are.

Photographs: Romany Travellers © Bert Hardy/Hulton Archive/Getty Images

Quotation: Takayuki Ikkaku, Arisa Hosaka and Toshihiro Kawabata,
Animal Crossing: Wild World, 2005 www.quotationspage.com

Just whistle while you work

Come on get smart,
tune up and start
to whistle while you work

Kangaroos are
the only large animals
to use

hopping

as a means of travel

Photograph: Kangaroo with joey
© John Giustina/Taxi/Getty Images

Somewhere,
over the rainbow,

skies are blue

And the dreams
that you dare to dream
Really do come true.

Photograph: A party of models boarding a plane to go to a beauty competition. © J A Hampton/Hulton Archive/Getty Images

Quotation: "Over the Rainbow" is a classic ballad song with music by Harold Arlen and lyrics by E.Y. Harburg. It was written for the movie The Wizard of Oz, and was sung by Judy Garland in that movie.

Life is either
a daring adventure
or nothing.

Photograph: The Governor-General leaves for
New Zealand - Royal Albert Dock - London
Viscount Cobham and his family leave England
on the liner 'Rangitiki'. 1957 © PA/PA
Archive/Press Association Images

Quotation: Helen Keller (1880 - 1968)
www.quotationspage.com

A man travels the world over in search of what he needs,

and returns home to find it.

Saying goodbye doesn't mean anything.

It's the time we spent together that matters, not how we left it.